Fun Comedy Skits Teaching Stage Directions

By D. M. Larson

This book includes three skits that involve very clear movement around the stage in order to teach new actors stage directions in a fun way.

"Pirates Stage Right" follows a crazy crew of pirates who have to push around their Captain and a tiny ship. For 5 or more actors (male or female).

"The Joke Olympics" skit presents the Matholypmics where mathletes compete, solving funny math problems. For 8 actors (male or female).

"Emotional Zones" is about two scientists trying to teach two androids how to feel emotions. For 4 actors (male or female).

You can use these skits as a springboard for additional learning. For example, students could make their own joke-olympics, practice emotions using stage directions to represent different emotions, or simply play a game of tic tac toe using a team of actors on stage.

SCRIPT 1 OF 3

PIRATES STAGE RIGHT

PIRATES STAGE RIGHT
(a skit about stage directions)
By D. M. Larson

<u>CAST OF CHARACTERS (5+ male or female)</u>
CAPTAIN ARR: rides around in tiny ship that other actors must push around
PIRATE BEE, DEE and WEE: 3 goofy pirates
PIRATE ZEE: Wants to be first mate and very loyal to CAPTAIN
(more PIRATES can be added)

(CAPTAIN is in a tiny pirate ship. PIRATES drag CAPTAIN DL and chant)

PIRATES: Down left, down left, down left!

CAPTAIN: Down! Down into the depths of the ocean.

PIRATE BEE: Down where, Captain?

CAPTAIN: Right down there.

PIRATE DEE: Way over there?

CAPTAIN: Right!

PIRATE WEE: We should have left it down here.

CAPTAIN: Right down there, crew. Down to the right.

(PIRATE chant as they move DR)

PIRATE: Down right, down right, down right!

(PIRATES drag CAPTAIN's tiny ship DR. They arrive and PIRATES are tired. CAPTAIN scowls at map and turns it around)

CAPTAIN: Arrrr! I had thee map upside down. Up there, mateys. Take me up there to the left.

PIRATE ZEE: Ay! Ay! Ay!

PIRATE BEE: Do we have to?

CAPTAIN: Set sail for the high seas!

PIRATE ZEE: Up to the left, crew.

PIRATE DEE: Is that starboard or port?

PIRATE WEE: Port is left.

PIRATE ZEE: Starboard is right.

CAPTAIN: There's no time to waste. Hard to port.

PIRATE BEE: Ready maties?

PIRATE DEE: Not really.

PIRATE ZEE: Push!

PIRATE WEE: Pull!

(PIRATE drag CAPTAIN UL and chant as they move)

PIRATES: Up left, up left, up left!

CAPTAIN: Well done, mateys. Well done.

PIRATE ZEE: Thank you, Captain.

PIRATE BEE: Are we there yet?

CAPTAIN: Nay! Our journey has only just begun.

PIRATE DEE: Are you serious?

CAPTAIN: Dead serious.

PIRATE WEE: Dead men tell no tales.

PIRATE BEE: What does that even mean?

PIRATE WEE: I'm not sure actually.

CAPTAIN: The map says we go 10 paces to the right.

(PIRATE ZEE takes 10 paces to UR)

PIRATE ZEE: Over here Captain?

CAPTAIN: Ay! Now take me over there crew.

PIRATE BEE: Are you sure?

CAPTAIN: Full speed ahead!

(PIRATE all move CAPTAIN to UR and chant)

PIRATES: Up right, up right, up right!

PIRATE BEE: Are we there yet?

CAPTAIN: We have arrived!

PIRATES: Huzzah!

CAPTAIN: Now… we go 10 paces starboard.

PIRATE ZEE: That's left.

CAPTAIN: Right now the middle!

PIRATE DEE: Left, right?

PIRATE ZEE: Right.

(PIRATES move CAPTAIN to R stage)

PIRATE WEE: Right!

PIRATE ZEE: No! Left!

PIRATE DEE: Right.

CAPTAIN: Left go!

PIRATES: Go left, go left, go left.

(PIRATES drag CAPTAIN to L as they chant)

CAPTAIN: Oh, wait. I had the map upside down again. It was right.

PIRATE: Go right, go right, go right.

(PIRATES drag CAPTAIN to R as they chant)

CAPTAIN: We're almost there!

PIRATE BEE: I was just gonna ask if we were there yet.

PIRATE ZEE: Where to next, Captain?

CAPTAIN: That's the spirit!

PIRATES WEE: There's always a Captain's pet in every crew.

PIRATE ZEE: I'm trying for first mate. That means I get to ride on the boat too.

PIRATE WEE: Then we have to drag two of you around?

PIRATE DEE: I need a new job.

CAPTAIN: Set sail for the high seas. Up the middle!

PIRATE ZEE: And straight on till morning.

(PIRATES chant as they drag CAPTAIN UC)

PIRATES: Up center, up center, up center!

CAPTAIN: We have arrived!

PIRATES: Huzzah!

CAPTAIN: Just one more…

PIRATE BEE: We're not there yet.

PIRATE DEE: This better be worth it.

CAPTAIN: Down below are hidden the stuff of dreams. Take us down the middle mateys!

PIRATE WEE: And this is it… for real this time?

CAPTAIN: Ay!

PIRATE ZEE: We can do it, crew!

(PIRATES chant as the take CAPTAIN DC)

PIRATES: Down center, down center, down center!

CAPTAIN: Well done, maties!

PIRATE BEE: So where is the treasure?

PIRATE DEE: Is it gold? Silver? Jewels?

PIRATE WEE: Chocolate?

CAPTAIN: It was something even better than all the treasure in the world. I have given you the treasure of teamwork.

PIRATE BEE: What?!

PIRATE DEE: I quit.

PIRATE WEE: Let's go to YoHo Yogurt. I'm hungry.

PIRATE BEE: We're out of here.

PIRATE DEE: Exit, stage right!

(PIRATE BEE, DEE, WEE all exit R)

CAPTAIN: Did I say something wrong?

PIRATE ZEE: Nay! They're just not cut out for this pirate's life like I be, Captain.

CAPTAIN: Take me to the center of it. Let me take one last look at what we have explored today?

PIRATE ZEE: Me? Alone?

CAPTAIN: Ay! Are you not worthy of this task?

PIRATE ZEE: I will try my best, Captain.

CAPTAIN: There is no try, matey. Only ay!

PIRATE ZEE: Ay! Center! Center! Center!

(PIRATE ZEE tries to drag CAPTAIN to the C and then passes out C)

CAPTAIN: Close enough. Now I sit in the center of it all, pondering the adventures we've had today, wondering what awaits up down below or up on the high seas. Yo ho, yo ho, it's the pirate's life for me.

(CAPTAIN looks dramatic and then sighs)

CAPTAIN (CONT.): Where's my Jolly Jelly Roll? I'm hungry.

END OF SCRIPT

UR upstage right	UC upstage center	UL upstage left
R right stage	C center	L left
DR downstage right	DC downstage center	DL downstage left

AUDIENCE

SCRIPT 2 OF 3

THE JOKE OLYMPICS

THE JOKE OLYMPICS
(a skit about stage directions)
By D. M. Larson

CAST OF CHARACTERS (8):
HOST: Named Plus Subset. Host of the Math Olympics.
VENNA: Named Venna Variable. Holds up signs to get audience reactions.
COUNT: Team X leader
2X: Team X mathlete
XSQUARED: Team X mathlete
INDIVISIBLE: Team Zero leader
NEGATIVE: Team Zero mathlete
RHONDA RHOMBUS: New mathlete who has never played before

(Stage is a giant tic tac toe board with each square representing stage directions)

UR upstage right	UC upstage center	UL upstage left
R right stage	C center	L left
DR downstage right	DC downstage center	DL downstage left

AUDIENCE

***

SCENE

HOST: Welcome to the Matholympics! This is where the world's top Mathletes compete to prove who is number 1. Two teams of mathletes will do battle to prove they are the sum total of greatness. Greater than the rest with no equal. But I'm off on a tangent. Let's add the players.

(AUDIENCE cheers as TEAM X enters. An assistant named VENNA can hold up an applause sign for the AUDIENCE)

HOST (CONT.): First we have Team X led by the Count.

COUNT: You can count on me!

HOST: Along with 2X.

2X: Double or nothing.

HOST: And X Squared.

XSQUARED: Get ready for an exponential victory.

(TEAM X gathers and cheers together)

ALL OF TEAM X: X marks the spot!

HOST: And now welcome the challengers, Team Zero.

(VENNA holds up a sign. AUDIENCE cheers)

HOST: The team captain, the Indivisible Zero.

INDIVISIBLE: Nothing will stand in our way.

HOST: Negative Zero.

NEGATIVE: We're zeroing in on a victory.

INDIVISIBLE: One of our top mathletes couldn't be here. She sprained her angle. So we brought in a new mathlete, Rhonda Rhombus.

(RHONDA enters, audience cheers and TEAM X looks smug)

COUNT: It's a noob.

2X: Maybe you should put on some glasses. It improves di-vision.

INDIVISIBLE: What's with the graph paper? TEAM X must be plotting something

XSQUARED: Team zero is like a circle. Totally pointless.

RHONDA: Are you going to play a complicated math game with equations or something?

HOST: We will play… tic tac toe!

(VENNA holds up a sign. AUDIENCE cheers)

RHONDA: Tic tac toe?

HOST: You will answer a series of math related questions. If you get the answer right, you select a place on the board for your X or O. Ready Count?

COUNT: Ready to be number one!

HOST: What's the prettiest shape?

COUNT: An acute triangle

HOST: Correct!

COUNT: X to C. Center stage.

(VENNA holds up a sign. AUDIENCE cheers. COUNT goes to C stage)

HOST: What's the warmest part of a room?

INDIVISIBLE: The corner. It's always 90 degrees.

HOST: Correct.

INDIVISIBLE: Zero to U-L, Upstage Left.

(VENNA holds up a sign. AUDIENCE cheers)

RHONDA: What's with all the weird questions?

NEGATIVE: The show wants the Math Olympics to be fun and wacky.

RHONDA: How am I supposed to know the answers to these riddles?

NEGATIVE: They still require logic and a knowledge of mathematics to solve.

HOST: Ready 2-X?

2X: Ready!

HOST: Why do you never argue with a 90 degree angle?

2X: They're always right.

(VENNA holds up a sign. AUDIENCE cheers)

2X: I'm going to U-R. Upstage right.

COUNT: Right on!

HOST: Ready Negative Zero?

NEGATIVE: Ready!

HOST: What is the smartest shape?

NEGATIVE: A circle. Because it has 360 degrees.

HOST: Correct!

(VENNA holds up a sign. AUDIENCE cheers)

NEGATIVE: I'm going to D-L. Downstage Left for the block!

(VENNA holds up a sign. AUDIENCE cheers again)

HOST: X Squared is up next.

X SQUARED: Let's solve this.

HOST: Why was the math book so sad?

X SQUARED: It had a lot of problems.

HOST: Correct!

(VENNA holds up a sign. AUDIENCE cheers)

X SQUARED: X to L. Left stage for the block!

(VENNA holds up a sign. AUDIENCE cheers again)

HOST: Next up, Rhonda for Team Zero

INDIVISIBLE: You can do it, Rhonda!

NEGATIVE: Let's win this!

HOST: Okay, Rhonda. Here is your question. What do mathletes do when it snows?

RHONDA: Um…

HOST: No help from the team or the audience.

RHODA: Let's see. Snow… math pun… um…

(VENNA holds up countdown signs and has audience count down)

AUDIENCE: 3, 2, 1.

HOST: Time's up. Sorry Rhonda. Team X has a chance to win. What is the answer team X? What do mathletes do when it snows?

COUNT: They make snow angles.

HOST: Correct!

COUNT: X to R. Right stage for the win!

(VENNA takes X card to R stage and holds it up. Team X members cheer. INDIVISIBLE and NEGATIVE go up to RHONDA)

INDIVISIBLE: It's okay, Rhonda. We'll win the next one.

HOST: Clear the board for game 2. Team Zero goes first.

INDIVISIBLE: Ready!

HOST: What do you call a hen who likes to count her eggs?

INDIVISIBLE: A mathmachicken.

HOST: Correct!

INDIVISIBLE: Zero to C! Center stage!

(INDIVISIBLE runs C. VENNA holds up a sign. AUDIENCE cheers)

HOST: Okay, Count. How do you make seven an even number?

COUNT: Remove the S.

HOST: Correct!

COUNT: X to D-R. Downstage right.

(VENNA holds up a sign. AUDIENCE cheers)

HOST: Negative Zero is up next.

NEGATIVE: I'll zero in on this answer.

HOST: What's the most dangerous shape?

NEGATIVE: The trapezoid.

HOST: Correct!

NEGATIVE: Zero to U-C. Upstage Center.

(NEGATIVE goes to UC. VENNA holds up a sign. AUDIENCE cheers)

HOST: Okay, 2-X. Here is your question. Which of your school supplies is always in charge?

(2X looks confused)

2X: Let's see. School supplies.

HOST: Looks like this one will be a problem.

2X: Wait… I'll get it.

(VENNA holds up countdown cards)

AUDIENCE: 3, 2, 1

(2X goes sadly back and X SQUARED gives a pat on the back)

HOST: Time's up. Okay, Rhonda. Here's your chance to steal and get the win.

(RHONDA goes to HOST nervously)

INDIVISION: We're counting on you!

NEGATIVE: You're the sum! You're the sum!

INDIVISION and NEGATIVE: You're the sum! You're the sum!

HOST: Let's have quiet. No help from the team or the audience.

(Everyone is quiet)

HOST (CONT.): Ready Rhonda?

(RHONDA is very nervous)

RHONDA: Yes, I'm ready.

HOST: Which of your school supplies is always in charge?

(RHONDA's face lights up)

RHONDA: The ruler!

HOST: That's… correct!

(VENNA holds up sign. AUDIENCE cheers)

RHONDA: Zero to D-C. Downstage center. For the win!

(RHONDA goes DC. Team Zero jumps up and down. VENNA holds up sign. AUDIENCE cheers)

HOST: We have an equivalent score between our two teams. Which will emerge the greater than of the equation? To find out we will have the two players who missed question do one final answer. 2X vs Rhonda Rhombus!

(VENNA holds up sign. AUDIENCE cheers. RHONDA is nervous)

INDIVISIBLE: Don't worry, Rhonda. You can do this!

NEGATIVE: You're the solution, Rhonda!

HOST: I will position myself downstage Center. 2X, please stand upstage left and Rhonda, please stand upstage right.

(HOST moves DC, 2X goes to UL and Rhonda goes UR)

HOST (CONT.): These two players will race downstage to DL and DR grab an answer from my hand.

(HOST holds out two cards with arms stretched out)

HOST: The first person to grab the card will read the answer and must come up with a question to go with it. Ready mathletes?

2X and RHONDA: Ready!

HOST: Go!

(VENNA holds up sign. AUDIENCE cheers. 2X and RHONDA race downstage. RHONDA grabs the card first and HOST snatches away card from 2X)

HOST: Read your answer and then you must come up with a question for it.

(RHONDA reads card)

RHONDA: Sum-mer.

HOST: You must now come up with a question.

(RHONDA looks confused. VENNA holds up signs for countdown)

AUDIENCE: 3, 2....

RHONDA: I got it!

(VENNA stops showing countdown cards)

RHONDA: What is a mathletes favorite season? Summer.

HOST: That's it!

(VENNA holds up sign. AUDIENCE cheers)

HOST (CONT.): Team Zero wins!

(MATHLETES all cheer for RHONDA and gather to congratulate her)

HOST: Thank you for joining us for the Math Olympics. I'm your host Plus Subset
And this is co-host, Venna Variable. Please join us next time where we'll play Rock, Paper, Scissors, Algebra, Geometry, Calculus!

(VENNA holds up sign. AUDIENCE cheers)

END OF SCRIPT

SCRIPT 3 OF 3

EMOTIONAL ZONES

Emotional Zones
(a skit with stage directions)
By D. M. Larson

CAST OF CHARACTERS (4 male or female)
ALPHA and OMEGA: Scientists
BEEP and BOOP: Androids who learn emotions for the first time.

(ALPHA enters L followed by BEEP, BOOP and OMEGA. ALPHA and OMEGA are dressed as scientists and carry electronic devices. BEEP and BOOP look human but have stiff robotic movements. They are androids)

ALPHA: Walk this way everyone. Follow me to the center. We have an exciting activity for you today.

(Everyone walk to C stage)

OMEGA: We are in place. Activating the emotional zones.

(BEEP and BOOP speak in a robotic, matter of fact way without any emotion)

BEEP: Emotional zones?

BOOP: This is new.

ALPHA: Yes, indeed. Very new and exciting.

OMEGA: We have developed a training ground so you can experiment with emotions.

ALPHA: You both have yet to grasp feelings, but this activity should help bring out those feelings in you.

BEEP: Feelings?

BOOP: Emotions?

ALPHA: Because you both are androids, you operate on pre-programed reactions to the world around you.

OMEGA: When someone speaks, you are programmed to look at them and make eye contact.

ALPHA: But how do you feel about what is said to you?

BEEP: I do not believe I feel anything.

BOOP: No, I do not either.

OMEGA: That is about to change. Activate the emotion chip protocol.

ALPHA: Activating the emotion chip protocol. Don't worry. This won't hurt a bit.

BEEP: We do not feel pain.

BOOP: We will be unharmed.

OMEGA: We shall see.

(ALPHA and OMEGA do some things on their devices and BEEP and BOOP close their eyes and bend over and lean on each as if they went to sleep standing up. Then they stand up again suddenly with their eyes open. BEEP looks around confused. BOOP looks around in wonder)

ALPHA: How do you feel?

(BEEP looks at ALPHA for a moment and makes a weird face)

BEEP: I feel… different.

BOOP: Me too. This is… most unusual.

OMEGA: The chips appear to be working.

ALPHA: Now when we stand in the center of our emotional zones, we are at peace. We are almost void of emotion, but in a good way. We are balanced.

OMEGA: But when you explore other areas of the grid, you will test out other emotions.

ALPHA: Beep?

BEEP: Yes?

ALPHA: I would like you to the left stage part of the grid. And Boop?

BOOP: Yes?

ALPHA: I would like you to step to the right stage part of the grid.

(BEEP goes to stage L and BOOP goes to stage R)

OMEGA: How do you feel?

BEEP: I feel… free… ready to explore. I feel excited. Like I could do anything. Huzzah!

(BEEP lets out a cheer)

ALPHA: Excellent. How about you, Boop?

BOOP: Hmmm… I feel secure. I feel calm. Protected.

OMEGA: Beep. I would now like you to go to the Upstage Left area.

BEEP: Right! Let's go!

(BEEP moves UL and jumps with excitement)

ALPHA: And Boop. Please go upstage right.

BOOP: Of course!

(BOOP goes UR and BOOP starts giggling)

OMEGA: Are laughing, Boop?

BOOP: Yes, I thought of something funny.

BEEP: A joke?

BOOP: In a way… yes.

BEEP: Oh! Please tell us the joke!

BOOP: I just realized my name sounds like Betty Boop. The cartoon character. What does she say? Boop boppy doo.

(BOOP and BEEP laugh. BEEP jumps up and down and claps. BOOP is laughing uncontrollably)

(ALPHA and OMEGA move UC)

ALPHA: This is going well so far.

OMEGA: Agreed.

ALPHA: Now both of you come upstage center.

(BEEP and BOOP go to them UC. Both are smalling but more calm)

OMEGA: How do you feel now?

BEEP: I feel… happy.

BOOP: Content.

ALPHA: Good. The middle of the two other emotions is just a simple happiness.

BEEP: I like this emotion best of all.

BOOP: I thought the laughing was fun too.

(They all go C stage again)

OMEGA: Not all emotions are good ones. We would like you to experience a wide range of emotions, even the bad ones.

BEEP: Why would we want to have bad emotions?

BOOP: Aren't the good ones better?

ALPHA: Everyone wants to feel good all the time, but it's important for our personal growth to experience bad emotions too. We learn from bad things more than good things sometimes. These challenges are what help us change and grow as people.

BEEP: If this is what we need to be more like people, then we should do it.

BOOP: I agree.

OMEGA: Excellent. We will have you both start downstage center.

(BEEP and BOOP go DC and start to look sad)

BEEP: I feel so sad.

BOOP: This is depressing. I don't feel very well.

BEEP: I don't like feeling this way.

ALPHA: I know feeling sad can be difficult. These are tough emotions to deal with.

BEEP: Do people often feel this way?

OMEGA: It depends on the person. Some feel that way sometimes. Some feel that way much of the time.

BOOP: This is terrible. If someone felt this way, I would want to give them a hug.

BEEP: I would like a hug.

(BOOP and BEEP hug and sniffle and cry)

BOOP: Thank you. I feel a little less sad.

ALPHA: That's excellent. You are finding ways to manage your emotions.

OMEGA: There's only one more set of emotions we'd like you to try.

BEEP: Are they worse than sad?

ALPHA: I'm afraid so. But these are also critical emotions for your growth.

BOOP: Then we will try.

OMEGA: Beep. You go downstage left. And Boop. You go downstage right.

(BEEP goes DL and BOOP goes DR. BEEP's face turns angry and BOOP's turns scared)

BEEP: Why are we doing this? I don't like this!

BOOP: Please don't shout. Please.

BEEP: But I don't understand why we have to do this? This is terrible!

BOOP: Don't get upset. I don't like it when you raise your voice.

BEEP: I can't help it! I have to let it out! I can't hold it in!

(BOOP falls to the ground and cowers)

BOOP: Please. Make it stop.

(BEEP runs over DR and grabs BOOP and takes her DC)

BEEP: Is that a little better?

BOOP: Yes, thank you.

BEEP: That was horrible.

BOOP: I don't like these bad emotions either.

BEEP: Which emotion did you like the best?

BOOP: The laughter. The funny emotions.

BEEP: Let's go then.

(BEEP takes BOOP UR. BOOP starts giggle. ALPHA and OMEGA move L and observe)

BOOP: I like it here.

(BEEP starts to laugh too)

BEEP: It is nice.

BOOP: What's your favorite emotion?

(BEEP goes UC)

BEEP: I like so many of them. Each one is interesting in its own way.

(BEEP goes UL. ALPHA and OMEGA move UC out of the way)

BEEP (CONT.): I love it actually! This is so fun!

(BOOP laughs at him)

BEEP (CONT.): I want to try them all again and again and again!

(BEEP runs around the stage in a circle from UL to L to DL to DC to DR to R to UR to UC. He runs around and around feeling each emotion very quickly and suddenly, changing as he hits each area. UL he jumps with excitement, L he cheers, DL he growls, DC he cries, DR he yelps with fear, R he hmms curiously, UR he laughs. He repeats this and BOOP points and laughs at him as he goes)

OMEGA: Is Beep malfunctioning?

ALPHA: It says all systems are normal.

OMEGA: This is not normal.

ALPHA: They do seem to be enjoying it though.

OMEGA: A little too much.

(ALPHA tries to stop BEEP. OMEGA gets BOOP and goes C)

ALPHA: Time to go now.

(BEEP is DL)

BEEP: I don't want to!

(ALPHA goes DL)

ALPHA: Come now, Beep.

(BEEP goes DC and cries)

BEEP: But I'm having so much fun.

(ALPHA follows to DC but BEEP goes DR and is afraid)

BEEP (CONT.): Don't touch me!

ALPHA: Please, Beep. I don't want to have to reset you.

(BEEP runs UR and laughs)

BEEP: Run! Run! As fast as you can. You can't catch me! I'm the robot man.

(ALPHA goes UR and BEEP runs UL)

BEEP: This is awesome!

(BOOP goes UL and cheers with him and they do high 5s)

END OF SCENE

UR upstage right (humorous)	UC upstage center (happy)	UL upstage left (excited)
R right stage (calm, secure, positive)	C center (at peace)	L left (adventurous, free)
DR downstage right (fear)	DC downstage center (sad)	DL downstage left (anger)

AUDIENCE